"Words of passion and wisdom that uplift and inspire, empower and motivate, awe and comfort, and help others through their journey of self-reflection..."

Memories of 2023

It Lingers On Within Me

AMY.B.GARRATT

Memories
of
2023

Memories
of
2023

It Lingers On Within Me

AMY.B.GARRATT

Happy New Year

Fresh coffee on the bedside table, the school run completed while I laid in bedsheet comfort. Slipping back into the warmth, I snuggle into my favourite arms and hands which stroke my hair. Nattering and giggles about nothing in particular, that shorthand we're so familiar with now. Smiles and forehead kisses, since I fell for a thoughtful boy. Early bedtimes are bliss, not the end of the day but a little bit of comfort when the hours have been long and a sedative to the fate of unforeseen stresses to come, when you have a spicy brain. We look to each other with our slow sleepy smiles, and our hands dance together in the dark of the peaceful sky.

Looking through the branches

Looking through the window, the buddleia arch curves against the sky. The butterfly lands on a stalk to take rest, and the blue tits sing their cheerful tunes. A love song for their wives and the dawning chorus of life awakening. They grasp at seeds left in offering from the humans who spy on them silently. They flit higher to enjoy a quiet meal, away from predators and their competitive friends. The mix of lavender fuchsia lilac and cream-coloured buds is a palette of night passing colours. I am a woman who knows the difference between the beauty of the flowers and the reliability of branches. On birthdays, the windowsill is decorated with gestures of affection. The vases filled with huddled crowded flowers, and the words of cards with best wishes and kind regards and heartfelt spilling over the edges of the paper. Cup of tea lifted to lips, as we watch the birds fly from their breakfast to the sun.

I Lick my Index Finger

I lick my index finger, to flick through the photo album pages of our memories… and this is what I see. The snapshot of our first date, we didn't eat nearly enough and 3 bottles of wine later we'd run through the first 20 years of our lives. I wondered if you'd stick around, especially when you discovered my hangover levels of h-angry or bedridden and pathetically anxious from the comedown. The first flowers you bought me on the next page, pressed into a book and then encased inside a photo frame to watch over us. Hard to capture the beauty of a living thing torn from the root, and a gentle sadness clouds over the end of a flowers life (if used purely for a generic valentine gesture). But this flower was a promise, a sentimentality that I didn't expect would last so long… and now it sits in the same room as my wedding photo, as a reminder for my whole lifetime.

Little Legs

Little legs skip along the path, free of the school gates and busy day of learning and play. She stops, tilts her head to the clouds and points at the 'pretty sky' above her. She catalogues the trees, the leaves, the sticks, the painted bike indicating the cycle lane, and simply states 'hand' when she wants to feel my palm. Her hair is wild, untameable and escaped strands are drifting in cool breeze, sneaking out of the carefully placed hair clips from earlier in the day. She giggles when she suddenly starts to run ahead, and shows a toothy grin when she wins the race. She runs around the back of me, and as I start to turn… she nips through my legs, like I am the bridge and she is the water of the stream. The laughter of something so simple, and yet so beautiful that it captures my heart so hard. She does this again and again, until she sees the path she wants to take, and she informs me where we're going. With her leading the way, we skip to nannies.

Watching My Mother

She stands with determined concentration, looking this way and that for symmetry, checking the end goal is in sight. She reaches up with tiny blades, and snips away the leaves from last autumn and parts of branches without life in them anymore. She steps back, takes in her work against the backdrop of sky and those watchful eyes from cars passengers as they pass by. The garden bin is filling up with the past year of growth, and making way for new shoots and new flowers to grow in their place. We carefully move around her orbit, being gentle not to stand on snowdrops beneath the tree, and watch as she crafts with her green hands. There are petals in her hair from reaching upwards, and they have showered her with the debris from her skilful artistry. She seems more at home in the garden, wearing her protective gloves, than anywhere we've been before.

Memory

Memory
is always
so precious
We hold it
carefully
in tight palms
And open
to embrace
remembrance.

Glass

A being made
of glass and some
transparent cliches etched
into this brutal world of pain, a
cage made of windows and projecting
images of people unaware they are so
privileged to walk in the fresh air, feel breeze
on their skin and see birds soaring overhead
in a joyfully contented memoir of everyday
miracles taken for granted…It is a glorious
moment in a rare occasion that I can step
outside of myself and join in with normalcy,
smashing through the walls and smiling
as I race away from inevitable pain.

Valentine

Somehow people manage… when I don't have the money to buy you dozens of roses, I will offer you a bouquet of truthful compliments. Financially, there's "never a good time to get married…" but even if we had a million pounds, the smile on your face at the end of an aisle would still be more precious and priceless to me, than any diamond could ever be. Anyone who ever made you feel insignificant, unloved, or that they "just weren't into you"… clearly never appreciated how your eyes glow like a sunset, when you share all the details about a nerdy topic that excites you. Call me old-fashioned, but I like to walk side by side holding hands and feeling the warmth of our pressed tightly palms. Call me unreasonable… but I never want to lose that magnetic force that pulls me to you, like the gravity of our world shifts each time we walk into the same room as the other… and we dance into each other's swirling orbits… my adoring stardust.

With a Pinch of Salt

With a pinch of salt,
with good humour,
at face value,
at first glance,
as it appears,
as far as you can tell,
by all intents,
by definition.
Take these words
from my wine cracked
open tongue and savour
the bitter aftertaste of
intoxicated blunted vowels.
On paper,
so the story goes,
by all accounts,
to the casual eye,
to the outside world,
as far as anyone can tell,
it appears to be the case,
that honesty is not always easy.

The Static

The static,
the crackle
of emotions
fizzing beneath.
Practiced faces
in the mirror
with smudged
mascara and
re-living old
mistakes in
real time.
Morning tea
tastes bitter
against new
brushed teeth
to scrub away
the taste of
last night's thrill.
The wind whistling
through the crack
in the crumbling walls.
This house has fallen

into neglect and the
wallpaper peels off
the cold plaster and
shows the old pencil
instructions for how
to decorate underneath.
I'm like these walls are
going to be… weirdly
fractured and unable
to hold the weight of
the shiny veneer on
top of my flaky skin.
Remember when we
were the architects of
our first attempt at
building love together…
When the cursive letters
curled around smooth edges
and your name tasted like
fearless ecstatic joy…

Show Me The World At Our Fingertips

Show me the world at our fingertips,
the breeze that carries the smell of
home and the leaves that part to
let the birds chirp through the day.
Paint me a picture of our future,
the hot air balloons filled with
possibilities and airborne ships
on their way to their churches.
Colour in the moon with yellow,
to compliment the sun and fill
in my complexion with a paint by
numbers or dot to dot my freckles.
Hold me close without saying anything
at all, and let your lips sleep beside the
sound of the ocean waves breaking in
a brand-new cadence of sound.
I am waiting for you to do all these things,
from here in the past while you live in my
future, I run to you while you wait for me to catch up…
so come find me.

Rabbiting On

Watching poets is a grand pastime.

Words of passion and wisdom that uplift and inspire, empower and motivate, awe and comfort, and help others through their journey of self-reflection. We hear humour and pain, light and darkness, all of us cheering for each other and applauding our efforts. The world is a better place for having poetry in it. I'm sure I'm better for letting poetry heal my wounds, and the pain cascading away through my outstretched arms, while I hold tightly to my inner peace. We are all human, and we are all the way we are… because of our deep experiences within existence.

For Lois

I throw my cloak of fake
self-confidence over my shoulders.
An imitation of a second skin
which contours and covers my own.
It flows easily over my still limbs
and pools neatly at my feet.
I'm covered from my neck
all the way down to my toes.
I turn to look at a reflection
and see myself from above.
A warrior who has been wearing
the wrong armour for all these years.
The critical voice inside my head
is silenced by the smooth fabric.
I flex my fingers and curl them
into the shape of a fist at my side.
There's really nothing better than
conquering layers of self-doubt.
Nothing sexier than beating the shit
out of your demons.

My Dress Has Pockets!

Inside a locket I kept an old picture,
And inside my frock are some pockets,
And a sweet wrapper from a trip,
To the flicks, a bus ticket from Scunny,
Home to the sticks!
Not many buses come out after eight,
And I put cold hands in my pocket and wait.
And the lady at the bus stop beams,
"Oh isn't that great!!"
And I beam "I know! I always celebrate…
When I find out a lovely dress, has lovely deep pockets.
Not pretend ones, sewn on for decoration,
I cheer and exclaim with deep admiration,
For the designers who gave us all what we're worth,
Us wearers of dresses and owners of skirts.
The one thing we want, we seek and desire,
And made me feel joyful when I did light the fire,
of my fashion statement determination…
This dress… it has pockets…
And they're a wonderful creation!

My Birthday Wishes

It's my party and I'll sleep in if I want to. Eat ice-cream straight from the tub and not worry about the calories. I'll swim until my arms get tired, and dive to the bottom of the pool to feel like a mermaid in an exhibition. I'll paint and draw and play with wool, crafting a new creation for my own sake. I'll walk through trees and fields of long grass, and breathe in the rain or the sunlight that pours through the canopy. I'll drink a bowl of iced coffee and dip cookies into the cloudy foam. I'll search through thrift shops for a new vase, and feel nostalgia for a special occasion to celebrate with flowers. I'll wear my most colourful clothes and not think on the stares or comments. I'll browse the bookshop shelves for a new addition to my aching to be read piles. I'll write a letter to myself, for all the hopes to come and all the dreams that have passed. I'll dance to 90s tunes, rave to 80s pop and thrash to 00s rock, and then curl up in a blanket to watch friends for the thousandth time. I'll drink my wine, brew my tea and breathe in a lungful of gratitude for my life and the next 12 months to come…

Favourite Things

Favourite things include
early mornings when we
can turn off the alarm and
listen to the birds sing through
closed blinds as sunlight peeks
inside. Coffee and pastries with
bare feet on warm kitchen tiles
and smiles with crumbs on cheeks.
Hot showers cascading or being
submerged in a bubbly bath of
warmth and comfortable luxury.
A glass of wine sitting in the
view of a hillside setting sun and
waiting for the constellations to
appear to us in a vision of nighttime
glory. The quiet of reading a good book
with no distractions or expectations,
filling our heads with dreamy stories
and beautiful pictures of fantasy life.
All enjoyed with your favourite person,
who can say everyone while saying
nothing, and just bask in the afterglow
of each other's presence.

Recognition

Starving for recognition is a painful thing. The cravings are often accompanied by an appetite for self destruction that is hard to resist. Unable to rest in this famished bed, my palpitating heart aches into my stomach. Twisting and shaking, the lace of my underclothes hangs from fragile bones. I am a ghost in the corner of your eye nowadays, a distraction from the worries that haunted you… and now they will haunt me forever instead. The cold water cannot slake my thirst and closure will only bring me closer to the end.

I Keep Your Words

The handwriting of
well wishes and hopes.
The birthday greetings
and Christmas cheer.
Good lucks and well done
congratulations and small
anecdotes on note paper.
Future endeavours in past
tense moments of peace.
The past has passed
and so have your hands
that can no longer write
me letters and cards and
stick stamps to envelopes
containing all the syllables
of words I can remember in
your unique tone of voice.
Remembering through a
bundle of now dead-end
communication, one way
telegrams of fondness held
inside a bundle and contained
inside a box…

Poetry Anthem

"God save our similes
We need hyperboles
Ridiculous Speech!!"

One

We are the ones. We lay our words on the page in an effort to understand ourselves. To understand the world that looks in on us. To try to figure out how we got here, and how we can move forward with our journey. We contemplate the future, we assess the past, we presently are undecided about most things in our lives. Our thoughts crash into us at 3am, and catch our breath through an unheard song lyric from years ago. We are creatures of habit, we are scribblers, and plotters. We are creatures who use our pages as a paperwork remedy. A balm to an old scar, a plaster covering the cracks of our former home. We are the ones who write our poetry, our stories, our lyrics, our music, and our everything… and we muse about how others could possibly understand it. Until we look up from the page, the notebook, the laptop, the napkin with a quickly jotted idea… and see someone nodding along. We have a connection with the world of words, a connection to readers near and far, because our words sow the seeds of a new meaning. Growth, as ancient as the clouds, and as warm as summer sunshine. As beautiful as sunrises or sunsets of all the past centuries, which guides our eager pen… or our dancing fingers on keys…

Breath

On the back of a sleeping neck.
The gentle to and fro…
Her breath is a lyric, only saints know.

Sinners

Causing sleepless nights.
Who bested her shining glory…
Sinners now absent, from this story.

Seances

I'm holding lonely seances in
these dim dull attic corners,
hidden from the daylight creatures.
Eager for spirits to answer my words
bubbling from my still beating heart
in this pre-corpse encounter.
Empty rooms below me listen
to my rambling questions of the
ghosts in long lost years of history.
The knocking on these walls sends
a chill through my body and mind,
and I regret my morbid desires.

Quiet

The smile on sleeping lips.
Hands across a rising chest…
Quiet contemplation she loves best.

Gaia

The green fern leaf is flowing through the waves of breeze, lingering above the canopies of trees. It bows in greeting, and waves to the fallen flower petals who used to live overhead. The brown from dirt and sandy paths, decorating with paw prints and past children's laughs. The purple white pink and red, of summers floral and glorious scent. Today tells us a fable of the forest, where the fairies hide behind closed doors. They scuff their shoes on tiny door mats, and wipe the earthy moments from their adventures.

Revolutionary

I am my own revolutionary. I will expand my own horizons. Embrace the chaos and the darkness. I will wave my own flag. The first one to include every colour. I am the rebel. The rebellion of my ancestors has left me feeling like a broken woman, left in the middle of a desolate nowhere. My mother was born in a small village, and my father was born in a rural town. I try to exist alongside a city where people ignore my words and try to change things by looking the other way. Revolution is a phenomenon, it has become more prevalent among young people who don't understand how things work, and are going through the stages of development… while we lay out Lego instead of real bricks…

Gothic

Be careful when you comb my hairs,
they're gothic to their roots…
and stand out like a silhouette,
against this toothy swift pursuit…
Seeking beauty in funhouse glass,
we form these masks of tragedy…
until irony seems too comical,
and sadness is a rhapsody…
an epic steampunk sonnet,
an aesthetic of romantic science…
and all of this you could simply tell,
from hair and combs' fleeting alliance…

Our Eyes Meet

Our eyes meet, they crinkle at the edges. The laughter lines are drawn from the sound of our voices. The words we hear are as loud as they are broad. We are the muses, who amuse ourselves with silly questions about how we feel, and who they think we are. The only reason we have such an open discussion… is because we were kept in cages. The doors opened and we flew for the very first time. They will make poetry of us, with this lovebird story. Loved and held, our feathers are smoothed with sweet caresses, and we chirp with pleasant gratitude.

Say My Name

Say my name...
In a gentle way that still
echoes in an empty room.
The hollow sound drawn from
those vowels and phrases,
as you curse those old gods,
for the pain caused by their vanity.
Say my name... when I am gone.
Taste the emptiness of the
lack of space I take up now.
Say my name... in quiet sorrow.
Until all names are forgotten.
See me now.
Not in the long ago,
the dazed and frustrated
who wanted just to forget.
See me in the morning.
Living in this future that I
prayed would one day exist,
opening my eyes to a fresh
start in a crisp breath of day.
See me now in the present.
In my wildest dreams that
are finally made real...

Tapestry

The cracks, the splinters,
across my aching chest,
my heaving painful breastbone,
my shattered kaleidoscopic heart
is cascading waves of light from
my dark inside to the blinding day.
This swirling darkness of twisting
prisms and obtuse images has
made my head spin like an old
spinning wheel making life's threads.
My mythology is repetitive attempts
at human connect, that are often cut
and knotted and torn and then removed
entirely from the tapestry I try to weave.
Yarn and weight are my main concerns
with that sequence of removing stitches
and trying to start afresh… but the paper
instructions are still always the same lines.
The light dims, I cannot work in shadows,
my kaleidoscope is not showing me those
same colours anymore… it is a hollow knight
and I'm not sure if I need to be rescued
anymore… or simply slain…

Autumn

Antique as the clouds,
the home of ancient rain,
within these darkened skies,
of pewter pencilled grey,
flies the clap of thunder,
after crackling electric waves,
in an unstable atmosphere,
to end these humid days.
We wipe our furrowed brows,
free of the summer sheen,
and stand beneath the water,
until we all are clean…

Chrysalis

The atmosphere is bent by humidity and rains down sapphires from heaven upon my scalp.
The ghosts of past days are curled inside grey magic clouds and whispering quiet lullabies.
My anxieties are cavernous and have set up home inside a hollow chest and stomach ache.
Releasing the pain is like leaving the door ajar so a moth can find the true light of the sunset.
It's crucial to remember that you can be reborn from a chrysalis and rise again in the morning.
Crawl into another body and gather your wits as storms pass through you.

Blooms

The woman I was is dead… yet
I still hear her voice inside my head.
Telling me to go and 'seize the day',
even when I cannot rise and play.
Mourning for every lost morning,
and each of the stolen afternoons,
each evening witnessing old blooms,
a bouquet placed by my deathbed.
I peek open one eye… recall the changing colour of the
sky, but all around me now
is shades of grey… this is what happens,
when you live inside yourself everyday.

Charged

Watching the forked light stretch across this midnight sky, the silent darkness is illuminated by crackling veins opening up the clouds. The momentary, rosy-lit skyline fades back to grey, and I listen for the whisper of the thunderclap... but only silence follows on. The heat is pressed into the ache across my temple, setting up residence in my skull from the swollen humidity of this night. I lay back on the pillow, and watch the display of power reaching towards the earth. An embrace of charged heat without a hint of loving warmth.

Sage

Sometimes I long for a clean slate,
a soul rinsed out with sage to keep
me free of bad spirits and sad memories.
My mind fresh and full of sweetness,
swimming through delicious ideas and
scented with halted honeycombed hair.
Dressed in Halloween dreams and decorated
with sugar skulls and punk rock booted feet.
My shape is still here, but my insides are
newly formed and more comfortable than before.
The corset I was pressed into has been unlaced…
and I can breathe more freely now.

Echo

Our lives are a prism of rainbow
colours reaching out into the universe.
Echoes of colour lasting forever beyond
the grave of scattered soil and prayer.
Our atomic clock is a reminder that we
are temporary creatures of nature,
that live and end like sunrise and sunset.
So kiss me like it's our last day and night.

Paper-chain

I am a paper-chain person, crafted within the curves and loops of scribbles across a blank notepad.
Cut out and viewed from a distance like the view of rain through steamed glass panes.
I write my darkest dirty damp feelings out onto the page, the words that many people think but won't say out loud.
I fold them into proud paper ships, and set them free.
Floating down this man made river caused by an overflowing street, they fall into a storm drain leading to the ocean.
I imagine my words out there, adventuring in the salty seven seas...'

Blossoms

It's one thing living up to your own expectations;
it's another living up to billions of strangers.
It's you that I want to hear about.
With an energy so much greater than the sparkle from
diamond decorated praise,
or the weight of grand marble columns
holding up these foundations sketched out
by distant architects.
The beauty of scattered blossoms is incomparable to those
laughter lines caught in a glance backwards at your
favourite ghosts, the memories of life before expectant
demands were placed upon you.

Discarded

Here we are once again, in autumn and
wearing my warmest September skirt.
Tugging at the loose thread, disconnected during a
rambling forest filled adventure.
I hoped this skirt had spacious pockets,
to store conkers, acorns, a stick shaped like a wand and I
was pleased to find much more.
A long skirt to swish past mushrooms, and trail through
the piles of fallen canopy, discarded from the naked and
now sleeping trees.
The time has come again, for the harvest before rebirth,
all of it riding on this hem of my skirt.

For HNDL

Camomile Yellow Orb.
Pale Chalked White.
Charcoal Grey Indents.
Blood Red Hunter.
Gigantic Super Sphere.
Curved Crescent Stone.
Ocean Blue Mastery.
Strawberry Tinted Harvest.
Longest Winter Chilled.
Bright Gleaming Silver.
Shades Of Moonlight…
A Global Delight.

Crimson

I take my autumnal days in crimson doses, as the scarlet leaves carpet the path laid out before me. I see the soft glow of light in early mornings, and the crisp breath of frost on the empty branches. I say farewell to this November, smelling of pumpkin spice and chai tea, and lean into winters strong embrace. Hallmark films showing the slopes of aspen, and hot chocolate under twinkling lights. It is time to decorate the fir, the spruce and smell the pine scented softness of December… glowing in candlelight and shining stars.

Yule

The logs are burning, as the people sing
cosy old carols, and shake bells that ring.
'I wish Yule a merry and joyful wintertide!'
as the wintery woods takes it all in stride.
Branches bow down, as if Odin followed by
overseeing the traditions of feasting & wine.
Carving the hides of the meat's sacrifices,
they make a toast raising high their vices…
Creatures watch from their dens & in nests,
the noise of the humans disturbing their rest.
A moths wings, attracted to warmth of light,
stumbles across this celebration of night…

Taste

I've got a taste for this
love language 'mutual respect'
& our most guilty pleasure
(by association) is watching
the enjoyment we each get
from the smallest of things.
Oh it does make me swoon like
some renaissance painted woman
when you spread out these options
that I just can't seem to refuse…
Blankets & snuggled close to you
with absolutely nothing else to do.

Headlines

Faces covered in this grey
dust like coal miners and
bleeding fingertips from
scouring the rubble at feet.
As hands heal and scabs
cover over the sins committed
our newly grown skin holds
onto the idea of a rainbow
lighting up the shadows.
The prospect of a happy ever
after seems to only exist now in
eyes grieving love stolen by hate…

One

One look…
at you across from me.
This quiet before the
declaration of intentions
and I know it's too late,
I'll be completely ruined by the morning.
One sentence…
I'll never be able to
accept less ever again.
I take your shaking hand
and call 'shotgun' to have
a shot at intertwining our silly heartstrings.

Past

I have so much sentiment inside
this careful heart that I wish it
would spill out of my subtle mouth,
& in the sweet syrupy words of
praise & gratitude I could casually
sprinkle myself with appreciation.
If loving myself wasn't an ordeal,
where I would feel selfish for not
tearing myself down & apart…
I could appreciate these kind of
'Rubenesque' hips & softness
beneath my prickly caged chest.

Present

Grief is inside this unopened gift.
Festive wrapping remaining intact,
the velvet bow is tightly bound
and the name is left unread…
Yet it lingers on within me,
summoned here by simple lyrics.
Tradition wafting through the walls,
to clothe this fallen tree in decoration.
Nostalgia without pain is a white lie…
a way to make it through the season.
But one day it will be the truth again,
and I will tear open the present tense.…

Future

Wait for me at the edge of this night.
In the crisp illumination of full moon light.
Not inside the glass of a sparkling toast.
Thirst quenched in words needed the most.
Every ending of year we're asked to choose…
Resolutions which fade like sugarplum bruise.
What kind of a promise could we even keep?
On this final tick of the years wintery sleep…
No clock hand could hold yours for hours.
Deliberate in slow motion love story of ours.
Every landmark from our story of yesteryear.
Ring out in these bells for another new year…

Connect With Amy

Instagram: @amybgarratt_author

Facebook Group: 'Rabbiting On Spoken Word'

Printed in Great Britain
by Amazon

47618355R00037